THE SKY HAS NOTHING BUT BLUE TO SAY

Poems by

Wayne F. Burke

Copyright© 2020 Wayne F. Burke
ISBN: 978-93-88319-23-2

First Edition: 2020
Rs. 200/-

Cyberwit.net
HIG 45 Kaushambi Kunj, Kalindipuram
Allahabad - 211011 (U.P.) India
http://www.cyberwit.net
Tel: +(91) 9415091004 +(91) (532) 2552257
E-mail: info@cyberwit.net

Printed at Repro India Limited.

Contents

sheets of river ice
the story of Winter
written on them

I wake to a crack of light
in the window and
croak of a crow outside
in sky streaked orange in the
east;
car headlights heat the
dark road
caw
ca
cold
red eyes of tail lights
fiery sun bleeds through
clouds that
douse the flames and
pronounce
a new
milk white day.

storm

the houses across the street
have disappeared
as has the street
and the cars have become shadows
of themselves
in white mist
of blown snow
in a sky
like a whitened sea
that has drown the ridge line
the mountain
the morning
and me.

walk

took a walk and
forced myself to
look at things;
hillsides, trees,
fences, cars, houses,
sky; I looked at the
black river, half-frozen;
at the ball field,
covered with snow;
at the playground,
empty; the swimming
pool, drained; the
ridge line, sparse;
the sidewalks, muddy;
the pigeons, in flight;
the flag, flapping;
the chimneys, smoking;
the lights, lit; the
night, moving-in;
the windows, golden,
the people within.

Washed-Out Sky

faded blue
silver jet moving through
to other time zones
new sky
a moon with a button-nose
god with four toes on
each club foot,
a meteor that
kisses the puckered sun
and the planet
Proxima b
(only 4.2 light years distant
btw) coming into
view.

Midnight Wind

say who
WHO
WHO!
Say whoa
WHOA!
Whoa-OH!
Say whew
WHEW!
Say
who-you?
Yeahass,
You!

Wraiths

a pale sun
and bushes crowding together
for warmth
as a relentless wind
scatters snow like sifting
sand
in a white desert—
a gray murk of
sky,
snow-dusted
hillsides,
whiffs of white smoke
over tiled roof tops;
the wind shreds the smoke
into wraiths
who scatter
and become ghosts
of the landscape.

On the Road

the trees in the park
got sick of hanging around
and they took off
en masse
to seek adventure
and almost every one
ended up
on a woodpile
somewhere
and even the ones who
survived the trip
found themselves
hanging-out
again
in parks
like the one
they'd left.

Future

seamless blue sky and
clouds floating in
like the future
taking their sweet time
in no apparent hurry
or worry about arrival,
departure, no struggle
toward a destiny
just a steady drift
to wherever the wind
takes them.

Street Corner

the sidewalk scene
a drag for
the lamp post
holding the flag
over curbstones bent out of shape
by the weather
and grout cracking-up over
something said by
the trashcan
to the hydrant,
a helmeted troll
guarding the portal of
manhole
to a world
seldom seen
because slabbed-over by
the cement.

Ra

the great telephone pole
offers the sun
two silver canisters
and other jewels
hung from golden threads
that stretch over the hedge
to a lesser pole
with a gray lozenge
unfit for the god
Ra
lying in a cloudy bed
its head
diademed
in clustered phosphorescent
shimmer.

Twilight Time

a smoky sky
and white slather,
the wooded hills brown,
the streets dark-gray;
twilight time
does something to me,
something good
to see a scrap of
crow
swoop to the woods:
it is not night
it is not day
a cornucopia of gray
cloud
with a spatter of charcoal bricks,
enough to start a fire
light the way
through
gathering darkness.

Sonata No. 10

telephone pole of ubiquity
leans over the Great Wall of China
hedge as
seagulls
with boomerang wings
soar
and sparrows dart
and black birds on
the wing
to and fro
below the sun
overrun by dolphins
and then
a whale.

Sonata No. 21

an ambulance screams into
view and
roadside trees with new green bud-dresses
wave;
cars and trucks carry-on as before
as ever
one after another;
the sky is silent
as always
nothing but blue to say;
the ridge line is
petrified; poor
trees,
cannot run from the ax
only clothe themselves
in green disguise.
The grass, the grass endures
and the breeze
which once blew down walls
ruffles the buds
and leaves
as the crow flies
but not nearly as high
as the hawk.

Deflation

the sun sinking in the West
and a jet plane heading straight for it—
a silver bullet
a needle
into the heart, an
arterial-centesis
and out spurts
magma
smegma
lava
cappuccino latte…
The deflated sun,
size of an air balloon,
means 20-degree days year round
and nobody in a good mood;
a planet of sour-pusses and
whiners, and
sunsets a streak
only
as if made by a small child
using a crayon.

row of sharks' teeth
on the eaves—
bite of the cold wind

Kalpas to Go

a howling baby
starts the world again
world without end
or beginning
we are born into
again and again
until nirvana when
all karmic debts
paid
the wheel of samsara
stops
to let off
a Buddha
while the rest
have kelpas to go
before arrival at
the golden silent hall of knowing,
beyond birth
beyond death.

Wing Tips

new wing tip shoes
on the table,
notebook on my lap,
symphony number
whatever by Franz
Haydn on the radio,
crescendo to climax;
my polyester pants
are black like my shoes
wrist watch hi ho
silver.

Pigeon

red-eyed, pink-footed
with goiter neck
luminescent green
spilled ink on its
pearl gray back
it comes down
off a roof, plebian
bird royal in flight,
chest out, one in
a line now of
bowling pins on the
roof-top of the Elks Club.

Such

2 crows swoop
into the ridge line
as a squirrel climbs
down a branch
and is chased by
2 others
along the expanse
of the bank's
frozen shimmer
the babbling river
cupcakes of
snow & ice,
sparkling water;
the crows, squirrels, river
and me,
we,
one suchness,
even the jet overhead
it's long needle
stitching us
and sky
together.

Sounds Like Snow

fat thick flakes that
obliterate
as they cover
or smother
the color of
the world
gone under snow
thick as a curtain
falling
from a milk-white sky
that has swallowed
ridge line and mountain
the great pine
half-hidden
the sound of a snowplow
pushing
spinning tires
unheard
since last December,
hey:
it must be
Winter.

Clouds

a fish with it's head
buried in gray murk;
a poodle behind it
and a squirrel
above
and a donkey the sun
burns through,
and the squirrel, now
a camel, and
the fish out
of a dark channel
sucker-mouth lips
opening to swallow
poodle and camel
both
who defend themselves by
becoming a horse's head,
one great blue eye
in place.

Translation

navigating the wet sidewalks
clumped with snow & ice
I reach the river of babble-on
murmuring, like
a crowd in a theater before
the curtain rises—
whispering, like
the children in bed before
lights out—
it babbles of wetness, no
doubt—
speaking in fluidities…
I cannot translate whatever
it speaks,
good thing I do not need to:
cannot translate the
croak of the crow
or
the screech of the wind
either.

Chorus

the crows are at it again
6 AM.
a great croaking cloud of
them
in the tree tops,
a non-stop chorus of
squawks
rising in crescendo to
climax, then
fading,
then rising
again
to herald-in
the new day
of dusky blue
and gray sky.

Morning Glory

gold folds in the East
the birds glide through
and white rolls West
in pastel-blue
background
and
peeping from
a dusky cloud the
eye of the sun
opening wide
bright areole
brighter yet the
first rays
across dark roof tops
dark streets
a golden promise of
some kind—
a brighter day—
a new Jerusalem on the horizon:
we cannot get there
because
too far away
but
hell, let's
start walking anyway
shall we?

Mouth

the running of the mouths
in the park today:
lip-flap
jaw bone
drone;
bushwha
murmur
drivel;
coming-in
fading-out,
flags on flagpoles
flap
too.

crow on a telephone line
cawing
an unlisted number

Laundry

6 crows wheeling through
a gray sky
one has something in it's mouth
the others are after
they chase each other around
a tree
with peeled bark like banana skins
and arms like frozen snakes;
Aw! Aw!
The drama unfolds outside the
laundry
where I wait
for my clothes
to dry.

Trestle

the train whistle calls me to
myself
and the local
green & yellow
glides past with motive force
as empty boxcars
behind the engine
pound across the
trestle
high above
a shimmering river of
white water ripples
closing between
pewter banks
brown & gold.

Glaze

sent a golden stream
into the golden-green
river,
in a big hurry
it seems
to deliver
itself downstream
in gleam & shimmer
to fall
in foamy splatter
then rising to
meander
down a channel
widening to
forever
after.

Slept Eight Hours Straight

and woke,
and went outside;
everything beautiful,
sparkling blue, electric
green,
fluffy white clouds,
and by the road
a dead beaver,
unlucky fellow
killed by a car
the day not so beautiful
for him
he is in beaver-heaven
now
building a log-jam
and has left the
bugs
deliriously happy,
such a stupendous
snack
never did they even
imagine.

Post Card

early morning light in the
east
blue patch behind Misty Mountain
mauve underbelly of steel cloud bank
turning rosy
smoke drifting from chimneys
of houses
steeple roofs jutting into
cauldron of
red sky.

gods

a gull
dull gray
like the sky
under which I sit
to pray
at the fountain
the new Kaaba
in the mini-park beside
the Chinese restaurant,
the living waters ripple
over the stone
like clock work,
a metronome,
moo goo guy pan
my prayer
to Allah
and all other gods
known and
unknown.

Touch the Sky

white moon in blue
sky, and
on the other side of the
valley
last rays of sun
above the ridge line
a saffron glow
that
slowly fades to
a purple haze
all through my
mind.

Totem

a great bird
with wings spread
flying above the
ridge line
a cascade of
bright white feathers
shimmering
silver-ed with age
dark gray breast and
eagle-eye of sun
glare
no one can escape
from the
unflinching orb
until it disappears
behind the lifting of
a great black wing.

April

standing by the
river, the gray & green water
cresting over rocks, a soft purling
flow
between pewter banks
brown & gold,
a woodchuck, handsome gray and
black, crosses a path
I walk
to the railroad tracks
and over the trestle;
admire the
view of the
river below
shimmering in the
sunshine and
rollicking around the
bend
to the stone bridge,
the deep shadow
beneath the arch
of granite rock,
a golden stream
it seems to me
and red the undergrowth
purple the trees,
sweet chirp of
birds in the
brush and
sweet air of
Spring.

Neon Green Trees

and electric blue sky
the single squid-eye of the
sun
casts shadows
beneath the trees
like pools
you can take a dip in
or hide from the heat in,
at least
until things cool
down.

Poem

dark green
ridge line
and one tree
stark outline
the one they hung
Tom Dooley from
in the gray
bleak
blook
of April
rain
on the doorstep
shroud in the sky
mist on the
mountain
fa
away
a long long
run.

Rain Drops

that dot
the freckled
sidewalk
and puddles with
bubbles and
rings
within rings:
bracelets
handcuffs
hoops of the Olympic logo
that ripple to
wherever
puddle meets
the street
full of sky
and cars
headlights like torches
on asphalt
spattered by
rain
forty days
and nights
brooks
running down the
gutters
a brown cascade
into catch basins of iron
fortitude
those who slog

through
need
too.

Twilight

and the city hushed;
a somber hue
of shadowed-ness.
Scars of the brick buildings
hidden,
wrinkles folded-in for night.
Black birds on the wing
beneath a charcoal sky
with pink ribbon.

Perfect

a blue infinitude and
dreamy clouds
above the sun
sinking down
to a horizon of
ridge line pines
marching along the crest
left right left
as a jet
coming in from the West
lays a stream of smoke
like a needle
to stitch a rent
should one appear
in the perfectly blue
sky.

A Leaf

brown
withered
torn
crawled up the
walkway to my
feet;
it did a little flip-flop
onto the grass
as two pigeons strut
like jail guards up
the walk
(looking for the leaf
I think)
and a squirrel came by
to speak to the pigeons
who nodded their heads
and looked in the
direction of the leaf
who
skittered off
in the nick of time.

Quorum

snout of a sturgeon
creeping in over the
tree tops and grazing
on distant broccoli mountain;
the wind blows the fish to
vapor, and a sea horse
appears, followed by a reindeer
in the electric blue sky sending
vibes down on neon-green
tree tops where elders gather
in a quorum, sage heads nodding
over the doings below.

Leaf Haiku

dare-devil leaves
leap off tall trees
and glide to ground

  suicidal leaves run
  out onto the highway
   beneath trucks

  dissolute leaves
  stick to the
  gutter

  yellow leaves cling
   to trees,
   afraid

  foolish leaves
  follow the mob
   up & down the street

Decay

of everything,
like the mailbox,
no longer blue but
gray,
like the fire hydrants
standing on the roadside
like truant children,
corroded with rust
paint-cracked
dust;
like the railroad tracks sunk,
in a gray street patched
like old clothes,
in front of the Thrift Store.

Gray Stone Walls

and slag heaps;
a crow with bow legs
strutting
like an old man
over by the garbage bin;
muddy streets
muddy rivers
muddled thoughts
about what I am
and am not
doing
here
on Planet Crouton.

October Afternoon

sky
black
baby blue
charcoal gray
streaked white
and full of specks,
birds, windblown leaves;
the hissing trees
jiggling
and a witch
with pointed hat
broomstick
shoots
like an arrow
behind the big pine
and goes down
somewhere
along the ridge line
and the air
turns ice-cold
and a mile-long train
of crows
ragged scraps
flap their fingered wings
over trees
blood-red and
tangerine.

1:30 PM.

mist and gray splotches of
clouds
swimming into the
dreary wonder of
a December afternoon
and settling down
among crenelated ridge lines
of black skeletal trees
like Transylvanian Vladimir
castles
fading in
fading out—
the misty ghosts of
Christmases.